CHOOSING YOUR DOODLE DOG

Labradoodle, Goldendoodle, Cockerpoo or another. What Doodle should you choose?

Katie Ann Bowen

Copyright © 2024 Katie Ann Bowen

All rights reserved

No part of this book may be reproduced, or stored in a retrieval system, or transmitted in any form or by any means, electronic, mechanical, photocopying, recording, or otherwise, without express written permission of the publisher.

Cover design by: Katie Ann Bowen
Printed in the United Kingdom

DEDICATION

This book is dedicated to Zorro, my Great Danoodle, Great Pane or Poodle x Great Dane mix, whatever you prefer. As big and lazy as a Dane, with the friendly demeanour of a Poodle, he was an amazing dog. He attracted attention wherever we went. People meeting him for the first time nearly always asked if he was an Irish Wolfhound. I can see why. In dim light and from the right angle, he looked like a werewolf. In fact, he was a big, lolloping, galumphing goofball of a dog. RIP Zorro. You are missed.

CONTENTS

Title Page
Copyright
Dedication
About this book
Introduction
Chapter 1: What makes Doodle dogs special?	1
Chapter 2: A brief history of Doodle dogs	3
Chapter 3: Doodle challenges and controversies	5
Chapter 4: Is "Doodle" considered a breed?	7
Chapter 5: Popular Poodle-mix breed names for Doodles	9
Chapter 6: What does F1, F2 and F3 generation mean?	11
Chapter 7: Are Doodles hypoallergenic?	13
Chapter 8: Caring for your Doodle dog	15
Chapter 9: Training your Doodle dog	17
Chapter 10: Showing your Doodle dog	21
Chapter 11: Buying your Doodle dog	23
Chapter 12: What Doodle should you choose?	26
APPENDIX 1: UK Doodle Breed Clubs & Associations	29
APPENDIX 2: US Doodle Breed Clubs & Associations	31
THANK YOU	33
About The Author	35

ABOUT THIS BOOK

Choosing Your Doodle Dog was born out of a love of Doodles of all kinds and a desire to share the reasons why they are wonderful dogs and companions. The book is meant to give would-be Doodle owners a glimpse into Doodles, their characteristics, quirks, challenges, and other factors to consider before welcoming one to your family. I wholeheartedly advise acquiring a Doodle from a responsible breeder or a Doodle rescue organisation. I am not a Doodle breeder.

INTRODUCTION

Imagine a canine companion with the intelligence of a Poodle and the boundless joy of a Retriever. Now make it inquisitive, friendly and irresistibly huggable. And add cute and adorable just for good measure.

Choosing a Doodle dog isn't just about picking a curly coat. It's about embracing a whirlwind of love, laughter, and adventure. Before you plunge headfirst into a sea of teddy bear faces, this book is your compass. A dive into the wondrous world of Doodles

What makes these cuties tick? Why are they the talk of the dog park? What are the unique charms and quirks that make Doodles unlike any other breed? From fluffy F1s to stylish F3s, decipher the generation code and find the perfect pup for your lifestyle.

But it's not all woofs and walkies. Are Doodles ethical? Hypoallergenic? Easy to train? How much do they cost? Hint: start saving now. Discover the facts behind the hype and make informed decisions.

This book is a one-stop shop for your Doodle destiny. Whether you're a seasoned dog lover or a first-time pup parent, this book has something for you. Grab a lead, a treat, open your heart and let the Doodling begin!

CHAPTER 1: **WHAT MAKES DOODLE DOGS SPECIAL?**

A Doodle dog is no ordinary dog. Doodles are whirlwinds of joy, loyalty and cuteness born from the magical mix of a poodle and another dog breed. It's a living confetti cannon of happiness, showering you with love and playful antics every day. But beyond the fluff and cuddles, there's more to the Doodle story. Here's a closer look at what makes them special.

Doodles aren't a recognised breed. They are a delightful mix of two already amazing breeds. The fluffy, intelligent poodle and other breeds like a Golden Retriever, Labrador retriever, beagle, or even schnauzer. This genetic mashup creates a unique combination of traits, with each Doodle having its own personality and appearance.

Think teddy bears crossed with fluffy clouds. That's the Doodle aesthetic. Their coats come in a rainbow of colours and textures, from bouncy curls to soft waves, and their eyes often sparkle with mischief.

Poodles are renowned for their intelligence, which is passed on to their Doodle offspring. These pups are eager to learn and love a challenge, making training fun.

Whether you're a city dweller or a mountain climber, your Doodle will be your shadow. They crave human connection and thrive on adventures, big or small, as long as they're by your side.

Doodles are adorable, playful, and intelligent dogs. If you're ready for an energetic, loving, and sometimes mischievous furry friend and can dedicate time to training and grooming, then a Doodle might be your perfect partner in crime (or cuddles). Remember, every Doodle breed and dog is unique, so get to know the specific needs of your canine companion and be ready for a lifetime of tail wags, happy barks, and unconditional love.

CHAPTER 2: **A BRIEF HISTORY OF DOODLE DOGS**

The adorable tangles of curls known as Doodle dogs may seem like a recent phenomenon, but their history weaves a surprising tale that stretches back further than you might think.

While the official "Doodle" boom didn't take off until the late 20th century, poodle crossbreeds existed much earlier. The Barbet, a curly-coated ancestor of the poodle dating back hundreds of years, likely mingled with other canine companions centuries ago, laying the groundwork for future Doodles.

In 1955, Sir Donald Campbell included his dog, Maxie, in his book "Into the Water Barrier". Maxie was a Poodle x Labrador and Sir Donald referred to him as a Labradoodle. It seems to have been a one-off and Labradoodles did not surface again until thirty years later.

In the 1960s, Monica Dickens, great-granddaughter of Charles Dickens, is credited with one of the earliest documented crossings of a Golden Retriever and a Poodle in 1969, aiming to combine the retriever's temperament with the poodle's low-shedding coat.

During the 1980s, Australian guide dog trainer Wally Conron sought a hypoallergenic guide dog for a client with allergies. His first litter of Labradoodles included three that were hypoallergenic. Later, his experiment sparked interest in the breed as a family companion.

Fast forward to the 1990s, and the "Doodle craze" exploded in North America, with various Doodle mixes like Goldendoodles, Labradoodles, and Cockapoos gaining immense popularity. Doodle awareness grew steadily in the UK, fuelled by positive media coverage and interest in their hypoallergenic qualities. Specific breeds like Cockerpoos and Schnoodles gained initial popularity alongside Labradoodles.

In the early 2000s in the UK, Doodle ownership started to accelerate, becoming more mainstream thanks to celebrity endorsements and the growing perception of Doodles as ideal family companions.

From the mid-2000s to the present, the UK Doodle craze peaked, with all Doodle breeds experiencing high demand. Concerns about unethical breeding practices also emerged, increasing a desired emphasis on responsible breeders and health testing.

The belief that poodles and their mixes are hypoallergenic and shed less made doodles attractive for allergy sufferers and families seeking low-maintenance dogs. More on that later.

CHAPTER 3: **DOODLE CHALLENGES AND CONTROVERSIES**

Major kennel clubs don't recognise Doodles, raising concerns about unregulated breeding and potential health issues.

In the UK's Doodle boom, unethical breeders exploited the surging demand, leading to puppy mills mass-producing pups in deplorable conditions, prioritising profit over animal welfare. Despite the potential health risks, some breeders focused solely on aesthetics like tiny sizes or lighter coats, so-called "designer dogs". Many ignored essential tests for genetic diseases, putting future pups at risk. Irresponsible advertisements with broad claims about Doodles' perfect temperament and low-maintenance care led to impulse purchases and later abandonment.

In fact, Doodles, especially those with retriever mixes, are high-energy and demanding. Walks, playtime, fetch sessions, and mental stimulation are essential to keep them happy and prevent mischievous chewing.

The gorgeous Doodle curls and waves don't stay perfect on their own. Regular brushing, professional grooming, and sometimes clipping are key to keeping tangles at bay and fur looking fabulous.

Doodle intelligence can sometimes translate to stubbornness during training. Positive reinforcement, patience, and a sense of humour go a long way in ensuring your Doodle is the perfect companion.

Despite the challenges, Doodles continue to be beloved companions worldwide. Responsible breeding, increased awareness about health concerns, and a focus on individual dog care have displaced unscrupulous commercial breeders. Hopefully, this will ensure these unique dogs continue as man's new best friend for generations to come.

CHAPTER 4: IS "DOODLE" CONSIDERED A BREED?

Strictly speaking, Doodles aren't a breed. They're a crossbreed. People refer to a Labradoodle or a Goldendoodle, but it is more correct to say these dogs are a Labrador-poodle mix or a Golden Retriever-poodle mix.

The UK's Kennel Club (KC) doesn't recognise Doodles as an official breed. They emphasise the need for more consistent characteristics and advocate for responsible breeding within recognised breeds.

Some UK vets express concerns about potential health issues related to the unpredictable nature of mixed-breed genetics in Doodles. They encourage responsible choices and highlight the importance of health testing regardless of breed label.

Responsible UK Doodle breeders often focus on specific Doodle mixes like Labradoodles or Cockapoos, striving for breed-specific health testing and promoting ethical breeding practices within these defined groups rather than advocating for broad "Doodle breed" recognition.

UK Doodle owners are passionate about their dogs, and many identify them as a distinct breed. They highlight their desirable qualities and advocate for responsible breeding and recognition of specific Doodle mixes.

Organisations like the UK's Doodle Owners' Club of Great Britain support mixed breeds and promote responsible ownership and Doodle breeding practices without pushing for official breed status.

Some media outlets and businesses in the UK might use the term "Doodle breed" for marketing purposes, even if not formally recognised by the KC.

While the "Doodle breed" debate exists in the UK, the focus is more on responsible breeding within specific Doodle mixes, prioritising health testing and ethical practices rather than pushing for official breed recognition by the KC. The UK discussion often highlights concerns about health and genetics related to mixed breeds.

Ultimately, the term Doodle holds various meanings for different groups of people in the UK, and the conversation will likely continue. I advise focusing on understanding the various perspectives and prioritising responsible ownership and breeding for all dogs, regardless of the official breed label.

CHAPTER 5: **POPULAR POODLE-MIX BREED NAMES FOR DOODLES**

Breed mashup names are a convenience that most Doodle owners enjoy. Goldendoodle is less of a mouthful than a poodle x golden retriever mix, hurts no one, and it's fun. There are some quite inventive names for poodle mixes.

Poodle x retriever mixes
- Labradoodle (Labrador retriever)
- Goldendoodle (Golden retriever)
- Groodle (Golden Retriever)
- BeagaDoodle (Beagle)
- Flatcoated retriever Doodle (flat-coated retriever)
- Curly-coated retriever Doodle (curly-coated retriever)

Poodle x spaniel Mixes
- Cockapoo (Cocker spaniel)
- SpringaDoodle (springer spaniel)
- Spoodle (Springer spaniel)
- Cavapoo (Cavalier King Charles spaniel)

- Brittany Doodle (Brittany)
- ClumberDoodle (Clumber spaniel)

Poodle x terrier mixes
- Schnoodle (Schnauzer)
- JackaDoodle (Jack Russell terrier)
- Westiepoo (west highland white terrier)
- Yorkiepoo (Yorkshire terrier)
- Wheaten Doodle (soft-coated Wheaton terrier)

Poodle x other hound/sporting Mixes
- Basset hound Doodle
- Bloodhound Doodle
- Pointer Doodle
- Setter Doodle
- Weimaraner Doodle

Poodle x other breeds
- Bernese mountain Doodle (Bernese mountain dog)
- AussieDoodle (Australian shepherd)
- Saint BerDoodle (Saint Bernard)
- Doodleman Pinscher (Doberman pinscher)

Some poodle mixes have a couple of different names, and some mix names have yet to gain widespread recognition. It really does not matter. You call your Doodle whatever you would like to. It must be right because there is no breed standard for Doodles. My own Doodle, Zorro, sadly long gone, was a Poodle x Great Dane mix. My kids referred to him fondly as a Great Pane or a Great Danoodle, depending on his antics and their mood.

CHAPTER 6: **WHAT DOES F1, F2 AND F3 GENERATION MEAN?**

When it comes to Doodles, generations matter. Understanding F1, F2, and F3 helps you navigate the world of these mixed-breed wonders so you know what you are getting. Here's a breakdown:

F1 Doodles are the originals. They're the first generation, born from breeding a poodle with another breed, like a Labrador Retriever, Golden Retriever, or Cocker Spaniel. Each pup is a unique blend of parent breeds with varying coat types, sizes, and temperaments. You might get a curly-haired, energetic Labradoodle or a calmer, wavy-coated Goldendoodle. It can be a surprise. Due to their newness and variation, F1 Doodles often command higher prices.

F2 Doodles are second-generation pups born from breeding two F1 Doodles or an F1 Doodle with a poodle again. The genetic mix starts to settle down, leading to more consistent traits within the litter. Coat types may be firmer, shedding reduced, and overall characteristics become more uniform. Compared to F1s,

F2 Doodles might be slightly less expensive due to less breeding uncertainty.

F3 Doodles are third-generation Doodles from two F2 Doodles or an F2 Doodle with a poodle. They represent a further refinement of the breed. Traits like coat type, size, and temperament become even more predictable within the litter. You can be more certain of what you're getting. Some consider F3s the perfect blend and their prices can vary depending on breeder reputation, coat type, and other factors.

F1, F2, and F3 are the most used terms to describe Doodle generations, but there are pups born beyond F3. For several reasons, F4 and F5 are less common descriptions. Around F3, Doodles tend to reach a relatively stable genetic configuration. Their characteristics, like coat type, size, and temperament, stabilise, making future generations offer less significant changes. Beyond F3, the terminology and exact breeding combinations become more complex and can lead to confusion for buyers and breeders, so it tends to go no further than F3.

After F3, many breeders transition to the term "multi-generational" to indicate ongoing breeding within the Doodle world without focusing on specific generation numbers. Breeders might diversify the gene pool by introducing other Doodle breeds or Poodles into the mix, creating multi-generational Doodles with unique traits. Through careful multi-generational breeding practices, some breeders aim to enhance specific desirable qualities, like hypoallergenic coats or calmer temperaments. Regardless of generation, responsible breeders prioritise selecting good breeding pairs based on health, temperament, and confirmation, not just generation numbers.

CHAPTER 7: **ARE DOODLES HYPOALLERGENIC?**

When it comes to Doodles and their hypoallergenic properties, the truth is a bit more nuanced than a simple yes or no. Here's what you need to know.

It is a myth that all Doodles are hypoallergenic. Some are more hypoallergenic than others, but none are completely hypoallergenic. While Doodles tend to be lower shedding than other dogs, there is no guarantee that Doodles won't trigger allergies. No dog breed is truly hypoallergenic. Allergies are often triggered by allergens in dog saliva, dander (dead skin cells), and urine, all of which Doodles produce, albeit typically in lower quantities than other dogs.

As such, Doodles can be a good choice for individuals with mild allergies. While not completely shed-free, Doodles generally shed less than many other breeds due to their poodle heritage. This can significantly reduce the quantity of allergens they produce. Regular brushing and grooming can further minimise dander and allergens by preventing loose hair and skin cells from building up.

Different Doodle mixes can have varying levels of shedding and dander production. Labradoodles and Goldendoodles might shed more than smaller mixes like Cockapoos or Schnoodles.

Some individuals might be mildly allergic to Doodles, while others might experience more severe reactions. If you're considering a Doodle and have allergies, try spending time with several before committing can help assess your reaction. Consult your doctor for allergy testing to understand your specific triggers and sensitivity levels. Choose a responsible breeder who prioritises health testing and ethical breeding practices, including testing for potential allergens. Very sensitive individuals can also try regular home deep-cleaning, air purification, and allergy medication to help manage their symptoms.

Poodles and Doodles aren't the only hypoallergenic breeds. Bichon Frises, Maltese, Shih Tzu, basset hounds, and several water dog breeds, among others, are known for lower allergen levels, though individual allergies vary.

CHAPTER 8: **CARING FOR YOUR DOODLE DOG**

Taking care of your Doodle is a delightful mix of providing for their physical needs and nurturing their playful spirit. Here's a guide to ensure your furry friend thrives.

Doodles come in various sizes, so you should tailor their diet to their specific needs. Consult your vet for guidance on the best type and amount of food based on their age, activity level, and breed mix.

These energetic pups need plenty of physical and mental stimulation. Daily walks, playtime, and outdoor adventures are essential to keep them happy and healthy. Consider activities like fetch, agility exercises, or even swimming if they enjoy it.

Regular brushing is crucial, especially for Doodles with curly coats, to prevent matting and tangles. You may need to get your Doodle clipped. Schedule baths every 4-6 weeks using gentle shampoos formulated for their coat type. Remember to trim their nails and clean their ears regularly.

Preventive veterinary care is vital. Schedule regular check-ups with your vet, including vaccinations, parasite control, and dental cleanings. Be mindful of common health concerns in their specific Doodle mix and discuss any potential issues with your vet.

Early socialisation and exposure to different people, animals, and environments are crucial for building confidence and preventing fear-based behaviours. Take them to parks, dog-friendly cafes, and puppy playdates to broaden their horizons.

Keep their minds active with puzzle toys, scent work games, and interactive training sessions. Consider dog agility or obedience training classes for an extra challenge and bonding experience.

Shower your Doodle with love and cuddles. They thrive on human interaction and playtime. Make time for walks, games, and simply snuggling on the couch for a happy and fulfilled pup.

Every Doodle is an individual. Observe their personality, energy levels, and specific mix to tailor their care and activities. Embrace your Doodle's joy and playful spirit, and together, you'll create a lifetime of happy memories.

CHAPTER 9: **TRAINING YOUR DOODLE DOG**

Doodles are intelligent and eager to please, making them responsive to positive reinforcement training. Use treats, praise, and playtime to teach them fun tricks and good manners. Be patient and consistent to ensure a happy and well-behaved companion. Their characteristics based on specific breed mixes might require some tweaks and tailoring of training techniques. Here are some pointers.

Channel their energy into engaging training sessions with games, fetch, agility exercises, and outdoor activities. Keep sessions short and varied to avoid boredom. Use fun tricks, clicker training, and puzzle toys to utilise their quick learning abilities. Keep training stimulating and challenging to maintain their interest.

Avoid harsh corrections and focus on positive reinforcement with treats, praise, and playtime. Early socialisation is crucial to build confidence and prevent anxiety. Tackle common concerns like mouthing by offering chew toys and redirecting attention.

Address barking through consistent training and identifying triggers. Overcome stubbornness by using engaging methods and setting clear expectations.

Knowledge of the breed mix can help inform training techniques. For poodle x retriever Doodles, focus on active training with fetch games, agility exercises, and obedience commands that involve movement. Spaniel mixes benefit from stimulating their love for sniffing with scent work games and treasure hunts. Keep training sessions short and engaging to avoid boredom. Channel the curious minds of poodle x terrier Doodles with puzzle toys, trick training, and obstacle courses. Provide consistent boundaries and training to curb potential territorial behaviours.

Doodles exhibit some common training challenges. Their keen interest in the world can make them easily distracted during training. Minimise distractions and choose quiet, calm environments for focus. Occasional bouts of stubbornness can surface, especially if they don't find the training engaging enough. Keep sessions fun and varied to maintain their interest. Pups of all breeds go through teething phases, and Doodles might explore mouthing with their playful nature. Provide chew toys and redirect attention when nipping occurs. Some mixes, like Beagle or Schnauzer crosses, can be prone to barking, requiring consistent training and addressing the underlying triggers for excessive vocalisation.

Each Doodle is an individual. Observe their personality, energy levels, and specific mix to tailor training methods and activities to their needs. You can build a strong, loving bond with your furry companion with patience, positive reinforcement, and understanding of their unique characteristics.

If you're experiencing difficulties with specific behaviours or need additional guidance, always consult a qualified dog trainer for personalised advice and support.

Good dog training practices work for Doodles as any other dog.

Positive reinforcement training is the gold standard for dog training, emphasising rewards and praise for desired behaviours. It's not about punishment but building a positive association between good behaviour and yummy treats, fun playtime, or even your enthusiastic "Good boy!" or "Good girl!" Here are some fundamental techniques for positive reinforcement training.

Clicker training uses a small handheld device that makes a distinct clicking sound. When your dog exhibits the desired behaviour, click the clicker immediately, followed by a treat or praise. The click marks the exact moment of the good behaviour, helping your dog understand what you're rewarding.

Luring uses a treat to lure your dog into the desired position or action. Gradually reduce the lure as your dog associates the movement with the reward. For example, to teach "sit," hold a treat above your dog's head, slowly guiding it backwards until its bottom touches the ground. Click and reward!

Capturing is rewarding your dog spontaneously when it naturally performs the desired behaviour. This reinforces the behaviour without any prompting from you. For example, if your dog sits on its own, click and reward immediately. You have to be observant and vigilant to be successful.

Shaping breaks down complex behaviours into smaller, more manageable steps and rewards each step progressively. For example, to teach "fetch," start by rewarding your dog for picking up the toy, then for taking a few steps with it, then for bringing it closer to you, and finally for dropping it at your feet.

Fading cues as your dog becomes proficient in a command. For example, gradually fade out the verbal cue "sit" and instead rely on hand signals, body language, or even just eye contact. This makes the communication more subtle and natural.

Socialisation is as essential for training as it is for the good care of your Doodle. A well-socialised dog used to new people, animals, places, noises and things is less likely to exhibit fear-based behaviours.

Exercise is essential. A tired dog is a well-behaved dog. Make sure your dog gets plenty of physical and mental activity. Keep your dog's mind engaged with puzzle toys, games, and training sessions.

Remember, training is a journey, not a destination. Enjoy the process and the bond you forge with your Doodle during training. By using positive reinforcement training techniques, you can build a strong, trusting relationship that makes training easier.

CHAPTER 10: **SHOWING YOUR DOODLE DOG**

While Doodles aren't recognised by major kennel clubs like the Kennel Club (KC) in the UK, there are still opportunities for Doodle owners to showcase their Doodles in several ways:

Many UK-based Doodle breed clubs, like the UK Doodle Breed Club, organise informal show-like events for Doodles and their owners. These gatherings usually focus on fun, community building, and celebrating the unique characteristics of different Doodle mixes.

Some dog festivals and events in the UK include Doodle-specific competitions like "Best Trick," "Waggiest Tail," or "Most Adorable Doodle." These can be a fun way to let your pup shine and win ribbons or prizes.

Specific organisations host "Dog Walks" or "Dog Shows" where all breeds, including Doodles, are welcome to participate. These events often raise funds for animal welfare causes and offer a chance for socialisation and friendly competition.

While Doodles aren't eligible for conformation shows under the KC, they can still participate in agility and obedience competitions held under organisations like the Agility Club UK or the Association of Pet Dog Trainers (APDT). These events focus on performance and training skills, offering a different kind of recognition for your Doodle.

Some independent crossbreed registries in the UK, like the International Designer Canine Association (IDCA), accept Doodles of various mixes. Registration through these organisations might provide limited recognition for your pup's pedigree, but it needs to be on par with official Kennel Club recognition.

The main purpose of these showcases isn't necessarily achieving championship titles or formal recognition for your Doodle. They're primarily about having fun, socialising with other Doodle owners, and celebrating the unique charm and companionship these furry friends bring.

To find Doodle events, check websites of Doodle breed clubs, dog event calendars like Dogging Around UK, or Facebook groups for "UK Doodles" or "[Your Region] Doodles" to find upcoming events.

Contact UK Doodle Breed Clubs directly to inquire about their events and activities.

Look for dog shows and festivals in your area and check if they include Doodle-specific categories or open competitions for all breeds.

Participating in events is entirely optional. Focus on finding activities you and your Doodle enjoy, whether informal gatherings, training classes, or simply exploring the outdoors together. The joy of a Doodle lies in their love and companionship, not the presence or absence of official recognition.

CHAPTER 11: **BUYING YOUR DOODLE DOG**

Doodle dog prices can vary significantly depending on several factors, so it's impossible to give a definitive answer. Expect to pay anywhere from £1,500 to £6,000 (one thousand five hundred to six thousand pounds) for a Doodle puppy from a reputable breeder. Rare mixes, exceptional pedigrees, or show potential could push the price even higher for the rarest Doodle mixes or pups with unique characteristics.

Labradoodles and Goldendoodles often command higher prices than some rarer Doodle mixes like Bernese Mountain Doodles or Basset Hound Doodles. This is because Labradoodles and Goldendoodles have been around for longer and enjoy immense popularity due to their reputation for intelligence, trainability, and friendly temperament. This higher demand naturally drives up the price. While Bernese Mountain Doodles and Basset Hound Doodles are gaining traction, their numbers are still comparatively smaller, creating a niche market with less consistent pricing.

Breeding Doodles with larger breeds like Bernese Mountain dogs or Basset Hounds can be more complex and costly, requiring special care for the mother and puppies. This cost is often reflected in the price tag. Smaller Doodles like Cockapoos or Schnoodles generally cost less.

Rare Doodle mixes might have smaller litter sizes, further decreasing overall availability and pushing prices up due to higher demand for the limited pups.

Rare coat colours or textures within any Doodle mix, common or rare, can significantly increase the price due to their novelty and desirability.

Pups from breeders with excellent reputations or those bred with exceptional conformation can fetch higher prices regardless of the mix. Also, responsible breeders prioritising health testing, ethical breeding practices, and proper socialisation typically charge more than backyard breeders.

It's important to note that price trends can vary depending on location. Certain regions might have a higher demand for specific Doodle mixes, impacting their cost.

While Labradoodles and Goldendoodles tend to be pricier, choosing a Doodle based solely on cost isn't ideal. Focus on finding a responsible breeder who prioritises health testing, ethical breeding practices, and temperament regardless of the mix or price tag.

Pups from dogs with show-quality conformation and temperament can fetch much higher prices than those from pet lines.

Breeding costs vary geographically, impacting puppy prices. Areas with high Doodle demand may see higher prices than regions with fewer interested buyers.

First-generation (F1) Doodles are often more expensive than

multi-generational crosses (F2, F3, etc.).

Older puppies or those with basic training might cost slightly less than young pups.

Don't forget to factor in additional expenses like food, vet care, and pet insurance when planning your Doodle budget.

Remember that price isn't everything. Finding the right Doodle for you is more important.

CHAPTER 12: **WHAT DOODLE SHOULD YOU CHOOSE?**

Choosing the perfect Doodle dog can be an exciting journey. Here's how to navigate the process and find your furry soulmate.

Start with Self-Reflection. How active are you? Do you live in an apartment or a house with a yard? Consider your daily routine and how much time you can dedicate to exercise and playtime.

Are you a first-time dog owner, or do you have experience with other breeds? Choose a Doodle mix that aligns with your comfort level and training ability.

Do you prefer a small, cuddly companion or a larger, playful pup? Think about the ideal size and energy level for your furry friend.

Are you comfortable with regular brushing and occasional baths? Different Doodle mixes have varying coat types and shedding levels, so consider your grooming time and cost commitment.

Explore different Doodle mixes like Labradoodles, Goldendoodles,

Cockapoos, Bernese Mountain Doodles, and more. Learn about their typical breed traits, temperament, and potential health concerns. Visit Doodle Breed Clubs and Associations. They offer valuable resources, breed standards, and information on responsible breeders. Connect with other Doodle owners online or in your community to get firsthand insights into their experiences and specific mixes.

Prioritise responsible breeders who employ health testing, ethical breeding practices, and proper socialisation. Look for breeders who are members of reputable Doodle associations. Schedule a visit to meet the breeder, see the puppies in their environment, and ask questions about their breeding practices and health guarantees. Observe the Puppies. Pay attention to the puppies' temperament, energy levels, and interaction with their siblings. Choose a puppy that seems playful, confident, and comfortable interacting with you.

Consider adopting a Doodle from a rescue organisation or shelter. You can find incredible pups who need loving homes and are often already house-trained and socialised. Remember, each Doodle is unique, regardless of their breed mix. Be open to their personalities and adapt your expectations accordingly.

Trust your gut feeling. Choose the puppy that resonates with you the most and feels like the perfect fit for your lifestyle and personality. Be prepared. Research puppy training, supplies, and veterinary care to ensure you're ready to welcome your furry friend home. Enjoy the journey. Embrace the joys of Doodle ownership, build a strong bond with your pup, and create a lifetime of happy memories together.

Choosing a Doodle dog is a big decision, but with careful consideration and research, you can find the perfect furry companion who brings endless love, laughter, and wagging tails into your life. Responsible breeding, prioritising health and temperament, and opening your heart to a deserving pup are crucial to finding your perfect Doodle match.

APPENDIX 1: **UK DOODLE BREED CLUBS & ASSOCIATIONS**

The UK Doodle Breed Club provides information on responsible breeders, health testing, and breed standards. They also host events and workshops for Doodle owners.

The Australian Labradoodle Association UK (ALAUK) is a resource for anyone interested in genuine Australian Labradoodles and lists approved UK breeders.

The Pets4Homes website lists Doodle puppies and adults available for adoption and purchase from breeders and rescue organisations in the UK.

The Rover platform connects dog owners with walkers, sitters, and boarding services, which can be helpful if you need someone to care for your Doodle while you're away.

Labradoodle Lifeline UK is a rescue organisation dedicated to rehoming Labradoodles, but they may also have other Doodle mixes available.

The Doodle Trust is a registered charity that rescues and rehomes all types of Doodles.

While not exclusively for Doodles, Battersea Dogs & Cats Home often has Doodle mixes available for adoption.

The Association of Pet Dog Trainers (APDT) provides a directory of qualified dog trainers in the UK. You can search by location and filter by training methods (positive reinforcement is recommended).

Many UK-based Facebook groups cater specifically to Doodle owners. These groups are great for sharing tips, asking questions, and connecting with other Doodle enthusiasts. Search on UK Doodle Owners or [Your region] Doodles. Regional Doodle groups may organise regular Doodle walks and meetups where you can socialise your dog with other Doodles.

Some Doodle breed clubs host dog shows and agility competitions specifically for Doodles. Participating in these events can be a fun way to bond with your dog and test their skills.

This is just a starting point. Many other resources are available for UK Doodle owners. Do your research, ask around, and choose the resources that best suit your needs and your furry friend's personality.

APPENDIX 2: **US DOODLE BREED CLUBS & ASSOCIATIONS**

The Goldendoodle Assocation of North America (GANAO is committed to the future of the Goldendoodle. It is the first and only breed club established for the Goldendoodle.

The Australian Labradoodle Association of America (ALAA) is dedicated to the well-being of the Australian Labradoodle and includes a list of breeders.

The Worldwide Australian Labradoodle Association US (WALA) includes a search-by-state list of breeders in the United States.

Many US-based Facebook groups cater specifically to Doodle owners. These groups are great for sharing tips, asking questions, and connecting with other Doodle enthusiasts. Search on US Doodle Owners or [Your region] Doodles. Regional Doodle groups may organise regular Doodle walks and meetups where you can socialise your dog with other Doodles.

Some Doodle breed clubs host dog shows and agility competitions specifically for Doodles. Participating in these events can be a fun way to bond with your dog and test their skills.

This is just a starting point. Many other resources are available for US Doodle owners. Do your research, ask around, and choose the resources that best suit your needs and your furry friend's personality.

THANK YOU

To my sister, Bronwyn, for introducing me to Doodles. Without her enthusiasm for these amazing dogs I may never have sought out Zorro. To my children, Bronya, Tom, Axana and Bethan, for keeping me fed when all I could think about were Doodles. And to my dogs Ziva, a Great Dane x Husky cross and Zebedee, a Plummer terrier x Parsons Russell cross. Their dinners have been later and their walks slightly shorter during the writing of this book. They agree I should get another Doodle.

ABOUT THE AUTHOR

Katie Ann Bowen

Katie is Welsh and lives in Shropshire on the Welsh border with several dogs and other animals. Currently, she does not have a Doodle, although they hold a special place in her heart. For many years, she shared her life with Zorro, a Great Dane x Poodle cross. Together, they enjoyed many adventures, including a six thousand mile trip across the United States and moving back to the United Kingdom after years abroad. She hopes to choose another Doodle very soon. This is her first book.

Printed in Great Britain
by Amazon